cle®

LEARNING FROM COACHING

How do I work with an instructional coach to grow as a teacher?

Nina
MOREL

ASCD Alexandria, VA USA

ASCD | arias™

Website: www.ascd.org   www.ascdarias.org
E-mail: books@ascd.org

Printed in the United States of America. Cover art © 2014 by ASCD. ASCD publications present a variety of viewpoints. The views expressed or implied in this book should not be interpreted as official positions of the Association.

PAPERBACK ISBN: 978-1-4166-1931-4   ASCD product #SF114066
Also available as an e-book (see Books in Print for the ISBNs).

Library of Congress Cataloging-in-Publication Data
Morel, Nina.
  Learning from coaching : how do I work with an instructional coach to grow as a teacher? / Nina Morel.
      pages cm. — (ASCD Arias)
  Includes bibliographical references.
  ISBN 978-1-4166-1931-4 (pbk. : alk. paper) 1. Mentoring in education. 2. Employees—Coaching of. 3. Teachers—In-service training. I. Title.
  LB1731.4.M67 2014
  371.102—dc23
                                                              2014014379

21 20 19 18 17 16 15 14   1 2 3 4 5 6 7 8 9 10

LEARNING FROM COACHING

How do I work with an instructional coach to grow as a teacher?

Want to earn a free ASCD Arias e-book?
Your opinion counts! Please take 2–3 minutes to give
us your feedback on this publication. All survey
respondents will be entered into a drawing to
win an ASCD Arias e-book.

Please visit
www.ascd.org/ariasfeedback

Thank you!

Introduction

Congratulations! You're embarking on an incredibly important journey with a colleague to help navigate the continual changes that are inherent in education. A coaching relationship, if entered into with thoughtfulness and intention on the part of you and your coach, can help you become and continue to be the best educator and leader you can be. This publication will deepen your understanding of the purpose of coaching, the teacher-coach relationship, and the responsibilities you have to each other.

You made the decision to enter what I consider the most challenging profession on Earth: teaching. Good teachers manage to cultivate deep personal relationships with their students while also demonstrating their content knowledge and pedagogical expertise in a very public setting. This in itself is emotionally and intellectually challenging. To complicate matters, though, new technology and research about the brain and learning continually impact and redefine "best practices" in the classroom. Teachers—who have very little time for additional study and training—are expected to implement these practices with expertise. On top of that, many teachers work in school environments with limited resources and have students with diverse linguistic, cultural, and economic backgrounds. Ultimately, teachers' roles require them to be excellent leaders and collaborators with colleagues, parents, administrators, and support professionals. This whole process takes place in a highly political environment of constant change.

Unlike other high-profile, challenging industries, the education field rarely has adequate support structures in place to help teachers navigate the professional demands they face on a daily basis. When I was hired for my first teaching job, I was expected to know (or be able to figure out on my own) what to do in the classroom, how to stay abreast of changes in best practices, and how to deal with any difficulties I might face. My principal made infrequent check-in visits and mandatory evaluative observations that felt more like a test of my ability than an opportunity for growth.

Absent an assigned mentor, I gathered my own. More experienced teachers in the building were kind enough to give the rookie a few tips and resources. As I became more experienced, though, those relationships became more social than professional, and I began to feel like a private contractor. This feeling was so strong that I considered leaving the profession; despite my hard work, I could not grow professionally like I wanted to.

This changed when I was introduced to instructional coaching. As a teacher, I began to see that I could solve almost any instructional problem if I had someone help me think about it through a coaching conversation. As a leader, I began to see how I could improve the quality of my relationships and performance using coaching skills. I discovered that I could have more effective parent engagement and productive parent-teacher meetings using the principles of coaching.

For the last few years, I have been teaching leaders and coaches how to develop instructional coaching programs. A recurring question from coaches and other school leaders is this: *We know coaching works, but how do we get teachers to choose to be coached and to make the most of it?* I think part of the answer is to invite teachers to prepare themselves for coaching by understanding it, reflecting on it, and then making the decision to use the process in their own professional growth. Consider this *your* invitation.

This publication reflects some basic beliefs about coaching:

1. Anyone who wants to excel and be the best at his or her chosen profession needs coaching.

2. Coaching is about helping you think more deeply about your work, organize your thoughts, set your own goals, and develop a plan to meet those goals.

3. Coaching is controlled by the teacher, not the coach. *You* are in the driver's seat.

4. Coaching is a relationship between two or more people, and all parties to the relationship are responsible for its success.

5. Coaching is confidential and based on trust.

Although there is a profession called coaching, there is also a coaching lifestyle that can benefit any leader, teacher, or parent. It is a lifestyle of asking instead of telling; listening more than speaking; and developing a deep, rich community with colleagues instead of superficial social cliques. This lifestyle is not just for professional coaches; it is for everyone who has the opportunity to coach or be coached in his or her personal and professional relationships.

The first four sections that follow deal with some major concerns I have heard from teachers:

1. What is coaching, and why is it important?

2. What is a coach, and what can I expect from him or her?

3. What is my role in the coaching relationship?

4. How do I make sure coaching is effective and productive?

The fifth section describes some problems that can arise and offers some suggestions for dealing with them. The Encore section at the end offers some additional resources that may be helpful as you begin your coaching experience.

What Is Coaching, and Why Is It Important?

Coaching is a general term used to describe a job, process, relationship, skill, model for professional development, and strategy for change in an organization. Because coaching can be defined so broadly, in so many different contexts, it's important to clarify what we are talking about when we discuss the word *coach* and the process of coaching.

The word *coach* has historically indicated "movement that is made easier." For example, you have probably traveled in a "motor coach," which is really just a fancy name meant to imply something nicer and more comfortable than a plain old bus. By the 19th century, the word had come to mean a tutor who "carried his or her pupils" through examinations. Since then, it has entered into sports, social services, the corporate world, and—more recently—education to refer to someone who helps others improve by way of a challenging endeavor.

As with all innovations in education, different schools and districts adopted or developed their own coaching models, which were variously based on the research of a growing number of educational authors and professional learning organizations. Today, the coaching model that most schools adopt includes a series of cycles in which the teacher asks the coach to observe a lesson in his or her room. The coach and teacher meet to discuss the teacher's goals and to decide on the focus of the observation.

For example, if a teacher is working on a new strategy to engage her English language learners in the classroom, she may ask her coach to observe and take notes on the level of engagement at different checkpoints in the lesson. The coach then observes and collects these data, either in person or by watching a video of the teacher "in action." After this observation, the coach and teacher meet again to reflect on the data and make a plan for the next step, which may include expanding, honing, or redirecting. At this point, the teacher may ask her coach to model a lesson or to coplan and coteach a lesson. Alternatively, the teacher may just bring an issue of concern to the conversation. It could be about how to engage parents more efficiently or how to work with a coworker more effectively. It's important to understand that the coach does not give advice or evaluate practice; he or she instead listens to the teacher and asks questions to help her think more deeply and clearly about the issue. In certain circumstances, the coach shares additional information and resources that are related to the teacher's goals.

Here is an example of a coaching conversation with a 3rd grade teacher who wants to talk with her coach about modifying instruction for a new English language learner (ELL):

Coach: Hi, Melinda! Thanks for reaching out to me. How are you today?

Teacher: Well, I'm OK, but I'm feeling overwhelmed. The principal just told me I'm getting a new preproduction ELL in my class tomorrow. I have a lot going on in my head trying to realign some things to make sure this unit is going to work for him. I'd just like to have more advance notice to plan for my students' needs. I've never even *had* a preproduction language learner before!

Coach: Wow, it sounds like you're stressed because you have ideas but don't have much time to adjust your plans! What do you know about instructional strategies for preproduction students?

Teacher: Not a lot. I think I remember from a workshop that a level 1 student may have a lot of receptive language but no productive . . . and they need time to listen and to learn basic interpersonal communication skills . . . BICS, I think it's called.

Coach: So you know you need to provide listening experiences and an introduction to basic communication skills. What has been effective in the past with your ELLs that might work with this student?

Teacher: Well, last year I had a student who came in at level 2, and we used graphic organizers and a word wall to help her understand academic language. I assigned her a buddy as well.

Coach: How did that work?

Teacher: Well, she progressed quickly. The word wall and graphic organizers are something I use all the time now. I'm just not sure that's a good first strategy for this student. I need to get him to the point where he can use the organizers. He is at the preproduction level, so I think I'll need some other ideas just to help him learn basic communication. The buddy is a good idea I can use, though . . . and I guess I can add some really basic school words to the wall. I can get pictures to represent *recess*, *art*, *music*, *lunch*, things like that. That could help him learn words he'll use every day.

Coach: Great! You're focusing on BICS and listening skills. So you have a first step—assigning a buddy—and some other solid strategies, like the word wall. What resources are you thinking about tapping into to get some other ideas for this student?

Teacher: Well, I have heard of Total Physical Response. That's a strategy where you act out words. Maybe I can call the district office and get the ELL consultant to come out and give me some information on that. I probably need to do an online search about preproduction kids. And maybe Mrs. Sherod can help me. She had several ELL students last year.

Coach: You have some strong options for new strategies. What's your plan? When do you think you can do this?

Teacher: I can call the district office right now, after our talk. I'll have an hour or so tonight to do some online research and get some ideas together so he feels welcome tomorrow when he arrives!

Coach: It sounds like you have clarified your plan. You have a call to make, some websites to review, and some lesson plans to modify! Would you like me to check in with you on Monday to see how it is going?

Teacher: Sure! Maybe by then I'll feel ready to have you observe me teach and give me some feedback on how engaged he appears to be. Then I can tell if the strategies I'm trying are effective.

Coach: Sure thing!

This conversation took less than five minutes, but it helped the teacher recognize available resources and make a plan. As you can see, all of the thoughts and ideas were the teacher's, and the coach simply helped her clarify her thinking and set a timeline. Over time, these conversations might get more sophisticated as the teacher explores deeper concepts related to planning for this student in her classroom.

If the coach is proficient in teaching ELLs, he or she might coteach, model new strategies, or identify and bring in relevant resources. Ultimately, the coach and the teacher may decide to lead a workshop for the entire faculty on the strategies they learned and implemented. Alternatively, the coach may facilitate a professional learning community (PLC) meeting in which the teacher collaborates with her peers to meet ELL students' needs and look for patterns that could help improve student achievement.

Increasingly, coaching like this takes place online or over the phone. With video technology becoming more accessible, more teachers are videotaping their lessons and sending them to a coach in another location. Though this can be an effective method to facilitate coaching across distance and time, it is important to note that the relationship between coach and teacher is critical and should never be shortchanged, regardless of what medium is used. In the pages to come, I'll offer more information about how to build the coaching relationship in both face-to-face and virtual settings.

There is strong evidence to suggest that coaching contributes to improved teaching and student learning. Almost 20 years ago, Joyce and Showers (1995) found that there was very little transfer of learning from the training room to the classroom. However, professional training that included theory, demonstration, practice, feedback, and coaching led to a positive transfer of new learning to the teacher's practice.

Since that research, multiple studies have shown that teachers improve their practice when coaching is part of professional learning. Several studies link coaching to learning transfer, teacher efficacy, teacher satisfaction, and student achievement (Biancarosa, Bryk, & Dexter, 2010; Bruce & Ross, 2008; Edwards, Green, Lyons, Rogers, & Swords, 1998; Joyce & Showers, 1995). Coaching has also been linked to a greater use of student data, an improvement in teachers' capacity to reflect, and the promotion of collective leadership across a school system (Annenberg Institute for School Reform, 2004).

The best evidence for a positive outcome resulting from coaching is through your own experience. If having a coach helps you think more deeply about your practice and your students' learning, if it helps you set goals and monitor progress for yourself and your students, and if it promotes celebration when you and your students meet your goals, then coaching has been a success and is effective for you.

What Is a Coach, and What Can I Expect From Him or Her?

This simple question is actually messy because "coach" can be a title that means many different things—and not all of them involve coaching! Sometimes a coach is actually a consultant, specialist, or facilitator who does not guide or instruct at all. In education, coaches spend much of their time planning, thinking, deciding, and reflecting with a teacher, but they also assume the role of an onsite professional developer who facilitates workshops and PLCs, teaches new concepts and strategies, and acts as a mentor to new teachers.

On the other hand, in some school settings, the people who perform these roles may have a very different title. For example, in some districts, all administrators are trained as coaches. Their title may be "principal," but their first role is that of coach because they believe the most important skill of leadership is coaching. Great leaders almost always use this as their first method to interact with teachers, parents, and students; they only use more authoritative communication when necessary.

Finally, in many schools, innovative teachers are taking it upon themselves to fulfill the role of coach, and they are coaching their peers in PLCs or in grade-level or subject-area teams. They are learning coaching skills together and practicing them with one another . . . and they're improving their teaching practice at the same time.

So, for our purposes, we will set aside job titles and think in terms of the role of coaching. A coach is your thinking partner. Ideally, he or she should be trained and experienced in listening carefully, observing closely, asking questions, and giving feedback that helps you reflect on your practice.

Look back at the example coaching conversation presented earlier. Can you identify instances of the coach directing, controlling, or evaluating the teacher? Hopefully you cannot, because these are the roles of a supervisor or an administrator—not a coach. Did the coach extend the teacher's knowledge and skills in any way? She could have suggested, "A preproduction student might be assigned a buddy or student peer to help him in the first days and weeks of school." If she had, she would have been teaching, not coaching. Remember, a coach is your peer—not necessarily an expert.

A coach may impart information when requested to, but this should not be the default stance of a coach, and it should be done only when you, the teacher, invite it. What if the teacher in the previous example was in her first year of teaching and had never worked with ELLs before or read about ELL strategies? If so, the conversation might look like this:

Teacher: Wow, I just got a new preproduction ELL student in my class, and I really don't know how to help him participate. I know I can do some research tonight, but in the meantime, do you have any suggestions to help me get through today?

Coach: You are asking me to give you a suggestion from my own experience, right? Well, it sometimes is helpful to give a preproduction ELL student a buddy to show him what to do during the day. The buddy can guide him, and sometimes the ELL student can just copy what the buddy is doing and begin to get a sense of the classroom. This also gives him someone to try to talk to without calling attention to himself. You probably want to think about this more tonight and refine how you would like to start out tomorrow, but that might be something that will help your student right this minute! I can also send you the links to some websites that have great overviews of strategies for preproduction ELL students.

It makes sense to look at the distinction between *mentor* and *coach* at this point. In many cases, a mentor is assigned to a new teacher or employee. A mentor is a more experienced person who guides or tutors a novice. He or she may have less teaching experience but more practical experience in the school, grade level, or content area. Many schools have excellent mentorship programs for new or aspiring principals as well. Someone can even be both a mentor to new teachers and a coach to more experienced teachers.

A coach is a professional peer who may or may not have more experience or expertise in teaching or the content area. Either way, he or she does not share that expertise in coaching sessions. Indeed, a coach might know nothing at all about the teacher's subject area. This is not necessarily a deficit, and it actually may make the coaching relationship stronger since the coach is not tempted to teach, mentor, or advise the teacher. However, an effective coach *does* have an area of expertise the teacher may not: he or she is trained in the skills of effective listening, questioning, observing, and giving nonevaluative feedback. In my experience, these skills are rare and difficult to perfect, but they are highly effective in helping a teacher grow.

What you can expect from your coach is strict adherence to the rules of professional ethics, such as those available from the International Coach Federation (www.coachfederation.org/about/ethics.aspx). This code stipulates that a coach must hold confidential all information from coaching sessions unless the teacher specifically agrees that it can be shared. The coach must be honest and professional at all times. You should also expect your coach to have your best interests and the interests of your students at heart.

What Is My Role in the Coaching Relationship?

Coaching is a relationship, and anyone who has been in a relationship knows that it "takes two to tango!" Coaches are usually quite good at building and maintaining strong professional relationships with the teachers they coach. Each teacher, however, also has a major responsibility for the relationship's success. As teachers, we are used to planning and delivering instruction to others. We may even use coaching practices in our own classrooms. Transitioning roles and becoming the person who is coached may seem unnatural for some of us. Therefore, it's good to know what we can do to make that relationship and process a success. This section provides some core ideas to help you get the most out of coaching.

Understand How You Learn

As adults, we learn differently than the children we teach every day. For the most part, we learn best when we have a vested interest in something, have a problem to solve or a challenge we want to meet, and then have the opportunity to practice within the context of our own work environment. Remember the so-called sit-and-get professional development sessions you've likely experienced at some point in your career? The presenter might have been entertaining and brilliant, but if you did not want to learn the information—and if you couldn't see how it would benefit your practice—it was more than likely a waste of time. If, however, that same session was the response to a need identified by your school, your team, or yourself as an individual, it could be invigorating. If you and your colleagues collaborated to create a plan to implement the new learning in your school, or if you had a coach observe and support you as you implement the learning, the information in the session could have directly impacted practice in your classroom (Joyce & Showers, 1995).

Adults, unlike children, already have a long history of learning, and we're each familiar with our own learning styles and preferences. We may already know whether it is more productive for us to read about a new strategy or watch it modeled before we try it out ourselves. You may feel more comfortable being observed by a coach than being videotaped. These preferences often influence not only how we learn but also how we teach, and they are important factors in our professional learning. Therefore, it's important to share your learning preferences with your coach as you discuss new teaching methods, familiarize yourself with learning standards, or plan to teach a new subject. Your coach may challenge you to stretch yourself and try new methods of learning and teaching, but this is a decision you can make after reflection about how it will affect your own learning and that of your students.

Try It, and Expect a Learning Dip

As adult learners, we want to try things for ourselves—in a comfortable and familiar setting—to discover if they work. The problem is that they may not work immediately and without effort. Think about those infomercials for household products that promise to change your life and make arduous tasks like dicing an onion easy and fun. Do you believe them? My guess is that you have a healthy dose of skepticism, right? As an educator, I've found that there's *nothing* that makes a challenging task easy and fun the first time you do it. Usually, the first time I try a new strategy that has any complexity at all, it flops. Why? I lack confidence, I lack expertise, and I tend to overthink what I am doing . . . so my attempt comes off as fairly amateurish.

This is called the "learning dip." Any time you try a brand-new strategy, things will probably get a bit worse than they were before. However, after you integrate the new learning into what you're already doing (perhaps slowly, in chunks), you begin to get the hang of it and become more confident. Your coach can also give feedback to help you revise and hone your practice, further strengthening your confidence. In addition, he or she can help you choose a strategy to meet an identified need, model its correct usage, help you plan how to integrate it into your practice, and then observe you and collect data you can review together. Your coach is aware that when you first use a new strategy, the process won't be flawless . . . but you have to know this as well. If you don't, chances are high that you'll quit when you experience the learning dip and never try again. We know this from other areas of our lives—if we fall off the bike, then we need to get right back on—but sometimes we have to remind ourselves that the same thing is true for our professional practice.

Demand Helpful Feedback

We need feedback in order to learn. I like the term *feedforward*, because good feedback should feed us with information we can use going forward. It shouldn't starve our souls with anxiety and blame about the past, nor should it simply provide affirmation of what we are already doing well. In a coaching relationship, don't accept "Great lesson!" without further information or explanation. You are not looking for a pat on the back; rather, you're looking for reflective, nonevaluative feedback that provides specific data that will improve your practice in the future. An example of helpful feedback might be, "When you transitioned from whole-group to small-group instruction, 20 of the 26 students were engaged and on task six minutes into the lesson." If your coach does not give you this kind of feedback, ask for it.

Be Willing to Identify the Challenge

Recognizing our need to learn things that solve our own (not someone else's) problems, we need to identify and articulate the professional challenges we face so we can work on them with a coach. When I coach, I like to ask teachers to identify their greatest strengths and their greatest challenges in the classroom. Almost without fail, the answer to this question reveals two sides of the same coin. For example: "I am great at spontaneity; I can really roll with the teachable moment. But my challenge is time management; I often struggle to get to the stated objective of the lesson."

In an evaluative culture, competition dictates that we promote our strengths and hide our vulnerabilities. In a coaching culture, we realize that our strengths and weaknesses often go hand in hand. Therefore, we embrace areas of challenge as places where we can learn and develop. Remember, challenges or perceived weaknesses are not static. For instance, I might have named classroom management as a strength until the year I had a student with whom my tried-and-true system just did not work. I felt so confident that I was doing the right thing, but my supposed "areas of strength" were actually limiting my perspective and keeping me from trying something different. Ultimately, I needed to set aside my ego and seek help from a coach to discover a new approach that would help me reach that student.

Get to Know Yourself

In Parker Palmer's (2007) classic work *The Courage to Teach*, the author writes: "As I teach, I project the condition of my soul onto my students, my subject, and our way of being together. . . . Knowing myself is as crucial to good teaching as knowing my students and my subject" (pp. 2–3).

Indeed, teaching is a profession that is so personal and intimate that if you don't understand yourself, then you cannot understand how you view your students or impact them. The process of coaching is one way to learn more about yourself, but the more you already understand and can share with your coach, the more productive your relationship will be. At the foundation of self-knowledge is your belief structure. Our beliefs are composed of what we think is true and what we base our decisions on. Typically, we view the world through the lens of these beliefs, notice data that reinforce the beliefs we already have, and ignore data that contradict our beliefs. We then add meaning to those data through our culture, personalities, and experiences.

We also have to understand what conditions help us do our best work. One of the most beneficial sessions I ever had with a coach was when we took a personality/learning inventory together. Doing so can increase awareness of yourself and shed some light on particular areas of conflict. For example, imagine a teacher who is very concrete and sequential in her thinking. She prefers step-by-step instructions and specific examples. She likes to know all of the relevant details and then use those to build the big picture. On the other hand, I think abstractly, organize thoughts globally, and must have the big picture before I can process the details. I like to experiment and improvise. In other words, the teacher always follows a recipe to the letter, and if she is missing an ingredient, she'll run to the store to get it. By contrast, I prefer to browse through the supermarket, choose ingredients that look good, and create a new recipe every meal. If I find I'm out of a particular ingredient, then I'll just substitute something else!

Needless to say, it's a good thing we don't cook together, but could we work together? As it turns out, we can.

Understanding this teacher's style helped me coach her. We learned how to work with each other very effectively simply because we each understood what the other needed. I knew I had to take her through all of the steps and *then* pull back and ask her about the big picture. She learned why I was driving her crazy by asking concept questions before she had identified the details!

There are many free or inexpensive inventories of personality, work style, values, and beliefs available online. Some are short and fun, and others take much longer and are more scientifically sound—but all are instructive. Taking one of these inventories as a group helps provide a common language to discuss workplace and professional needs. Your faculty may wish to do this, but if not, it is worth doing on your own. I think you'll find this self-knowledge will help you work more effectively with your students, colleagues, and coach. In any case, it will certainly give you valuable data to share with your coach as he or she is helping you set and meet professional learning goals.

Give Your Coach Grace

Let's face it. No one is *always* at the top of his or her game. Your coach may have more or less expertise and experience than you do. Even if your coach is excellent in every way, we all have bad days when we don't handle situations as we know we should. As professionals, it is our job to support one another in our roles and settle conflicts in productive ways. Of course, gossiping and complaining is unproductive and unprofessional in all cases, but it is even more so in the potentially powerful and vulnerable relationship of a teacher and his or her coach. Just as you must hold each other accountable for confidentiality in your relationship, you must also address problems and concerns about the relationship while face-to-face.

There are ways to handle significant problems (some of which we will discuss in the Troubleshooting section), but most conflict is manageable when both parties respect each other and the teacher-coach relationship. An important coaching concept is to *always assume the good intent of the speaker*. This means that, in any relationship, you should presume that the intentions of the other person are positive—even when you disagree. This does not require you to ignore poor behavior, but it invites you to approach all interactions with the idea that everyone wants to be effective and productive and that other outcomes are purely unintentional.

Believe That No One Sucks

"No one can learn from you if you think that they suck" (Aguilar, 2013, p. 33). In other (less colorful) words, you can't teach or coach people you think are incompetent, and you certainly can't learn from someone you view as incompetent. When I was a child, *sucks* was a forbidden word. As a high school teacher in the late 1990s and early 2000s, however, I began to hear it more and more from my students as they worked in their peer writing groups. I would overhear "My paper sucks," "No, it sucks a little, but not much," and "Well, it isn't great, but it doesn't suck." I worked with my students to come up with more precise language, but I began to understand their definition. If it sucks, it just sucks, and nothing can be done about it. This reveals a mental model that many of us have: if you're not already a great student (or teacher or coach), then you have no hope of change, and I can do nothing for you and you can do nothing for me. I am appalled that this belief worms its way into my brain, even though it goes against everything I know about teaching and learning. It's a belief that is antithetical to a collaborative school culture, it's the veritable death of a coaching relationship, and it's disastrous for student learning and teacher efficacy.

So how do we banish this model from our brains? I believe one way to combat this is by replacing criticism with gratitude. What do you truly appreciate about your coworkers, boss, students, or coach? What about yourself? I find the more time that I put into listing the things I appreciate, the more I realize that I don't believe *anyone* sucks . . . and the more I realize that *I* don't suck either!

Experience Coaching as the Coach

Coaching is not just for a special set of people. It's a leadership skill we can all use to great effect with our students, the parents of our students, our peers, our administrators, and even our own friends and family. The more you experience coaching, the more you'll be able to use the communication strategies and habits of mind to help others think more deeply and reflectively. Try coaching others and you'll get more out of your sessions with your own coach.

How Do I Make Sure Coaching Is Effective and Productive?

Coaching is like teaching. To make sure it's effective and productive, you must have a goal; a way to assess progress toward that goal; structure and norms for your experience, time, and space; and a way to celebrate when you meet your goal.

Making Goals and Assessing Progress

In coaching, the goal belongs to you, the teacher. You may be faced with wider school or grade-level goals—for example, meeting a certain proficiency level on a state test or implementing a new reading program—but what *you* do in *your* classroom to meet that goal is entirely up to *you*. Perhaps your principal has told you that you need to improve your classroom management or time on task in the classroom. Your coach can help you reflect on that feedback and create a personal goal to address it.

"But wait," you say. "I always get top scores on my evaluations, and my students are performing well above expectations. What kind of goal should I be working on?" My experience is that the most successful teachers are the ones who need coaching the most. Maybe you want to push yourself to a higher level of excellence, maybe you want to do your work more efficiently so you'll have more time for other priorities, or maybe you want to improve your leadership skills so you can help your colleagues. All of these are actual examples of goals I have worked on with excellent teachers as they strove to perfect their craft.

Your coach will likely keep data pertaining to your coaching interactions. Your school may do a climate survey before coaching begins and then again at regular intervals to assess effectiveness. You may be asked to complete surveys about your coaching relationship and its impact on your practice. Students in your class may be surveyed before and after coaching. Whether or not these formal assessments are in place, conducting your own action research will help you know whether the coaching experience is working for you. The easiest way to collect these data is through journaling.

Take a few moments after every coaching session to clarify your thoughts about the experience, record the goals you set for yourself, and identify ways you've grown. Doing so is an incredibly valuable practice in your own professional development. As a bonus, looking back over your journal to see how far you've come is a delightful treat when you're feeling discouraged. Don't have time to journal? You may wish to create a chart on which you regularly jot down the dates, goals, and outcomes of each coaching session. Coaches will often take notes or fill in graphic organizers during the coaching session and then leave them with the teacher at the end of the conversation. It's a good idea to keep these in chronological order and take time to go back and identify goals you succeeded in meeting.

One of the best ideas I've seen is when teachers model their own learning goals and experiences for their students and then let students help assess their progress. For example, one teacher shared with his class that he was learning to teach with problem-based learning, a new strategy for him. He explained that he had been studying and researching this type of teaching and learning and was working with his coach to improve himself. He believed that this approach would help the class learn math concepts more easily. He asked his students to remember that when people learn something new, they tend to make mistakes and need a lot of encouragement. He was no different. His coach would model the strategy, and then he would try it. The students were asked to provide feedback on his performance in their daily journals. Later in the unit, he gave his students surveys of incremental progress toward his goals. Through this process, the teacher modeled how responsible adults approach problems, and the students learned how to offer constructive feedback and support—powerful 21st century skills.

At times, your goal might be something quantifiable. Perhaps you have an instructional goal you can assess via test scores, or perhaps you want to decrease the number of disciplinary actions you need to take in a week. Your coach can help you gather and reflect on these data. One of the many roles of a coach is to simply be another set of eyes in your classroom. At your request, your coach may observe a lesson and record time on task, teacher wait time, student movement, questioning methods, opportunities for student feedback, nonverbal communication—almost anything you might want to improve. Your coach should give you the data he or she collects and help you set a reasonable goal; then, together, you can compare your scores over time or even with different groups of students during the day.

Documenting individual progress toward your goals helps your own sense of self-efficacy—the feeling you get when you know you can reach a goal. There is another purpose for keeping records of coaching interactions, though, and that is deciding whether coaching is worth the investment in time, resources, and personnel. Teachers who feel their professional growth is supported by coaches often communicate with parents, administrators, school board members, and other community stakeholders about their successes. Having data to back up these opinions is powerful when tough decisions about allocating scarce resources must be made.

Structuring the Coaching Interaction

Coaching interactions differ from casual conversations in many ways, but one of the most important is the structure it takes. There are many different protocols (procedures) for a coaching conversation, but all of the models have some similarities. They begin by identifying the norms and goals of the conversation, and then they clarify thinking about the situation, identify options, and declare a commitment to the next steps in addressing the challenge. For example, the GROW model can be recorded on a graphic organizer with four sections (Whitmore, 2002): Goals, Reality, Options, and Will. First, the coach and teacher identify the goal. What does the teacher hope to achieve? Then they identify the reality. What is going on now, and what are the obstacles to reaching the goal? Next, the coach helps the teacher identify options for action. What are some different ideas that might help the teacher solve the problem and achieve the goal? Finally, the teacher chooses which one item he or she wants to focus on first and, together with the coach, decides what he or she will do. This next step might be an observation or a lesson modeled by the coach, or it might be a conversation the teacher wants to have with a student or parent, an area to reflect on more privately, or a strategy to try in the classroom. The teacher and coach make an agreement to meet again to follow up on these actions. If the teacher wants to be observed, a date is set for the observation and for the post-observation conference.

For the structure to be successful, it's very important for the coach and teacher to be committed to the time frame they agree upon and to avoid rescheduling coaching appointments in all cases except emergencies, especially at the beginning. It's like exercising. When you first get started and don't yet see the benefits, it's easy to put it off or bail out at the last moment. However, if you commit to stay with it until you begin to see results, there is no way you'll want to miss a session!

Regardless of the length or location of a coaching conversation, both parties need to agree to and follow a set of norms (or agreements) around the conversation. This process is much simpler in a one-on-one coaching interaction than it is in a team situation, but it is no less important. The teacher and coach must agree to the duration of the discussion, the system of scheduling and rescheduling appointments, and—most importantly—the degree of confidentiality of the session. One norm concerning confidentiality might be that the coach will agree not to discuss what happens in coaching conversations in any other setting, even with the person who is being coached. It is imperative that the coach and teacher begin their relationship with a conversation about confidentiality in which these issues are agreed upon. The norms should be revisited at every coaching appointment, and there should be a discussion about their continuing effectiveness every six months at the very least.

Making Time

Time is something no one seems to have enough of, and "lack of time" is the number-one reason teachers say they fail to collaborate with their colleagues. I maintain that because we have so much to do and so little time to do it in, we *must* collaborate. Effective administrators recognize the importance of time, and they protect professional learning and collaboration time. In other words, they recognize that teachers need protected time to coach and observe one another.

Innovative schools that have implemented structured schoolwide coaching programs have thought outside the proverbial box of their daily schedules to build in time for collaboration. Some schools have built a master schedule to include common planning periods (perhaps with all students in a given grade or subject in "specials" at the same time). Others look for times when students can be supervised by fewer teachers or by noninstructional staff (e.g., during tests, films, field trips, presentations by guest speakers, or independent reading time) and rotate these responsibilities so different groups of teachers have time to work together. Some districts "bank" time by extending the school day by a few minutes and then starting late or ending early one day a week. Others have replaced faculty meetings with e-mails or videocasts and used the "found time" for collaboration. All of these plans are especially effective for peer coaching, group coaching, professional learning communities, shared planning, and team data analysis. If you are fortunate enough to have someone in your building who is assigned to coaching all day, it is also relatively easy to schedule a few minutes before or after school, during a planning period, or even during a lunch period.

Whether your school is "time wealthy" or "time poor," you still want to be frugal and spend every moment as effectively as you can. Your school and district have gone to great effort to create and protect time for the important business of professional learning. Using it wisely and showing results justify this sacrifice.

You and your coach will have to decide on how long your coaching conversations will last. Usually, they are 15–30 minutes, but they can be as short as 10 minutes. I find that it is much more productive to have short, focused, and frequent conversations than it is to have long, infrequent conversations. After the intense concentration of 15–30 minutes, both coach and teacher usually have more than enough to do and think about before they meet again. As you both get better and better at the process, your conversations might get shorter.

The coach should begin each session by establishing the time you will stop, and it is his or her responsibility to stick to the schedule. If time is up and you both feel it necessary to continue, you can agree to extend the conversation for 5–10 more minutes. Be cautious, though, because many times lengthening the conversation brings less instead of more clarity to the discussion. Stopping and agreeing to reflect before meeting again at another time may be a more beneficial use of time.

Coaching, once you get the hang of it, actually saves time. A good coach can help you organize your thoughts so your planning is more efficient. He or she can help you cut through the weeds to see the real issue and help you address it effectively. A good coach can help you identify options when all you see are the obstacles. Consider the following example, which actually comes from my own experience coaching a teacher who was having difficulty with a parent who regularly sent her long, complaining e-mails about the school dress code, the class policies for discipline, the amount of homework the teacher assigned, and her grading procedures. In our conversation, the teacher revealed that the e-mails made her feel defensive and insecure, and she spent long hours crafting written responses to each criticism the parent lobbed her way. When she addressed one concern, it seemed that another one would immediately pop up. As her coach, I listened, and the last part of our interaction was as follows:

Coach: You're annoyed that this one parent is taking up a lot of time that could be better spent planning your lessons. You believe the parent is just a complainer who, as soon as one thing is handled, thinks of another problem to point out. As you have reflected on your interactions with this parent, what did you decide the parent *really* wants from you?

Teacher: Hmm . . . I guess I never thought about what she wants. I guess I figured she was just doing it to make my life more difficult! [*laughs*] But if that is all she wants, she sure is putting a lot of effort into it. . . . You know, when I think about it, I guess she's just worried about her kid. She wants someone to know she cares. She wants someone to listen to her frustrations and fears.

Coach: Wow. That is an amazing discovery. You're saying she really wants someone to "witness her struggle" as a parent . . . to listen to her.

Teacher: Yes. I don't know why that didn't occur to me.

Coach: As you think about that, what are you planning to do?

Teacher: I'm going to quit rebutting all her concerns. I'm going to e-mail her—or better yet, have a conversation—and tell her that I hear her: that I know she's frustrated with the system sometimes, that I know she has a lot on her plate, and that we can work together to make sure her child succeeds in school.

When I followed up a few weeks later, the teacher had followed through with her plan, and she felt she and the parent had begun to establish a productive working relationship.

Better yet, the time spent on the e-mail responses had dropped to almost zero. When complaints did come, she paraphrased the parent's concerns, showed her that she cared, and thanked the parent for her input . . . all in just a few moments, in contrast to the hours of rebuttal writing she had done before. The teacher could have eventually figured this out on her own, but her emotions were clouding her thought processes. She just needed someone to paraphrase what she was thinking, ask her some reflective questions, and let her come up with her own answers. She would have gotten there eventually, but 10 minutes of coaching sped up the process exponentially.

Making Space: Face-to-Face or Remotely

Coaching takes place in time and space, and it is imperative that you have a private, uninterrupted space for coaching. Space like this is at a premium in a school. I get that. Many coaches I know have laminated signs that say "Coaching Session in Progress," which they place on a classroom or office door to indicate that no interruptions should occur. In schools new to coaching—where teachers are not yet comfortable with their coaching being public—the signs could say "Conference in progress. Please do not disturb."

Phone or video coaching creates a virtual space that allows for even greater privacy, and it enables coaches to help teachers and leaders across much wider geographic areas. Coaching via phone or videoconference also brings some extra challenges, however. One thing your coach wants to do is listen and watch for your emotions and passions around the issues you discuss. Your coach is trained to observe your body language and tone of voice and to help you identify your personal goals and aspirations. On the phone or via video, this process can be more difficult.

Teachers have to be patient with coaching in virtual settings until the coach becomes familiar with their tone of voice in different states of emotion. You might have to be more vigilant about correcting your coach's paraphrases than you would in a face-to-face setting. In a recent phone coaching session, I admitted, "Since I can't see your body language, I'm having trouble gauging your reactions to my paraphrases of your statements. Please correct me if I misrepresent your emotions, and feel free to help me out with sounds (whoops, hollers, or groans) as I paraphrase." This added some humor, helped us both relax, and gave the teacher permission to be vocal in her reactions to what I was saying. If you feel that your coach is not on the same wavelength during a phone or video coaching session, try paying attention to and vocalizing your own body language. You might say, "Yes, yes" to indicate you strongly agree or "Hmm" if you don't really understand or are not sure you agree. Sitting in complete (polite) silence while your coach talks may inhibit the usefulness of his or her comments, paraphrases, and feedback.

Celebrating Successes

Have you ever worked incredibly hard to accomplish something, finally gotten it just right, and when you turned around for the applause (either real or figurative) . . . no one was there? This happens all too frequently to teachers. Only you know how hard you worked to get Carl to sit in his seat for a whole lesson, or to get Melia to read an entire page without stumbling, or to get the whole class to understand the difference between *mitosis* and *meiosis*. Then, suddenly, they do! Your colleagues and administrators may care, but they are not in the classroom with you and likely did not plan the lesson with you. They are elsewhere in the building experiencing their own private triumphs and struggles. You rush home to your family, and they smile and nod. Maybe they just don't get why it is a big deal.

Your coach will get it. If your coach played a crucial role in your planning and reflecting processes, he or she will feel the same success you do. Coaches know the value of these successes and how much work teachers put into them, and they *want* to celebrate those successes. Trust me. As one coach told me, "The teacher and coach share a special relationship, because both see what happens in the classroom. The principal and other teachers get a quick snapshot, but only we have the full picture of the growth that has been going on."

Celebration not only feels good but also is necessary if you want to sustain good work and have more successes to celebrate. One of the fundamental roles of a coach is to be a cheerleader who supports you when you're struggling through a difficult implementation period and who celebrates with you when you meet your goals. While you are in the "learning dip," it can be tempting to accept failure and give up. Your coach will remind you to celebrate the incremental successes (and failures) that are necessary to achieve full competence. Celebrating the failures—"Yeah! We tried that, and it didn't work! We took a risk and learned something!"—reinforces the fact that taking a risk is a part of the learning process that should be rewarded.

Your role as the teacher in the teacher-coach relationship is to share your successes and failures with your coach and open yourself to a celebration of both. You are part of a larger school culture that most likely needs more celebration. Working with your coach to create celebrations both big and small for your class, team, and school can go a long way toward promoting a positive school culture.

Troubleshooting

As much as we hate to admit it, the coaching relationship has as many potential pitfalls as any other human relationship. The following are some representative vignettes of issues that concern both coaches and teachers.

Can These Relationships Be Saved?

Garrett met with his coach at his new school for the first time, and he was excited about the experience. When he walked back down the hall to his classroom after their meeting, however, he got some startling information. He learned that his coach's niece was going to be in his class this year.

Garrett's experience is not unique. In many districts, it is all but impossible to avoid this potential "conflict of interest." Variations on this vignette include coaches or teachers who are related or are close friends of principals, superintendents, or other school personnel who supervise the coach and/or teacher. Are such situations actually conflicts of interest? The answer, of course, depends on whether both the coach and the teacher feel they can still have a productive relationship. As soon as the coach discovers a potential conflict, he or she should reveal that conflict to the teacher, and vice versa. A frank conversation about how the outside relationship might affect the coaching relationship—and the level of trust and confidentiality you should expect—are key to making this situation work. If at any time, however, either party begins to feel the relationship is counterproductive, it is best to end the coaching relationship and seek another coach.

David was furious. He had just completed a conference with his coach, and she asked him if he wanted some help with his writing, because she found some errors in his lesson plans they were reviewing. He felt insulted that he, a seasoned teacher, would be criticized for his English grammar.

If your coach gives you feedback that you find painful or confusing, make sure you understand it in the way it was intended and let the coach know how it affected you. In all likelihood, you and your coach are viewing the comment very differently. The coach means to be helpful but has instead been unintentionally hurtful. Giving good feedback can be hard, and coaches (like everyone else) sometimes mess up. If your coach makes a similar mistake, consider taking responsibility for your reaction and ask for clarification.

In this example, David might have replied, "I hear you saying you don't think my writing is acceptable." The coach might have said, "Oh, no! Not at all! I apologize . . . I didn't intend that message from my comment! Let me rephrase." In other words, David's paraphrase would have shown the coach that she had been unsuccessful in her communication. Transparency can help avoid any miscommunication that impacts the working relationship.

How Close Is Too Close?

Sarah was excited when her best friend Monique got the instructional coaching job at her school . . . until she realized that Monique would now be her coach! She had always profited from working with Bill, her previous coach, but now she was wondering if coaching would work with Monique given their close friendship.

Teachers frequently form close bonds and friendships with their colleagues, and when a teacher's role changes to coach, there is often an understandable amount of anxiety. Nevertheless, it's been my experience that you can be coached by and coach your best friend! If anything, the relationship may become stronger. Coaching is a peer relationship—not a supervisory one. Therefore, it's much easier to remain close when your friend becomes your coach than it might be if your friend were to become your principal or supervisor.

Of course, there are a couple of potential pitfalls to be aware of. The first is that others might feel that the coach gives preferential treatment to his or her friend. It is up to both parties to make sure the coach allocates his or her time to all teachers on an equitable basis. Second, friends might fall into unproductive social patterns of discourse with each other during coaching sessions—chatting, venting, or gossiping rather than listening, paraphrasing, questioning, and giving reflective feedback. It's important to differentiate coaching from socializing. It's a good idea to find shorthand ways of identifying whether it is "coaching time" or "social time." For example, a friend might walk into my office and preface a comment with either "I need you to coach me right now" or "OK, let me tell you something. I don't need you to coach me on this." It may come as a surprise, but most coaches will tell you that coaching skills and strategies have improved their relationships with friends and family.

When Is Coaching Not Enough?

Marci had been meeting with her coach for several weeks. The first few sessions went well, and Marci was able to create a solid plan to move forward with her goal of implementing guided reading groups in her classroom. However, when her coach followed up with observations, none of the details of the plan had been implemented. In the post-observation conference, Marci shared that she had been extremely depressed and had not been eating or sleeping well. She had lost weight and had no appetite. "Sometimes I just don't want to get out of bed in the morning. I barely have energy to get through the day," she confided.

Many of the principles of coaching come from the field of counseling. However, it is very important to remember the distinction between coaching and counseling: counseling often looks back at what happened and investigates the reasons why it happened; coaching, on the other hand, is about looking forward. A coach helps you see where you are today, articulate where you want to be, and develop a plan to get there. In this example, Marci knew what she wanted to do, and she had a good plan, but she just couldn't seem to motivate herself to do it. She had other issues that went beyond the need to reflect on and plan for her professional practice. Marci's coach reminded her how much she cared for her and gently advised her to seek counseling for her situation. Remember, your coach is not a trained counselor. It is not his or her job to work with you on emotional or psychological issues that are impeding your work performance. If you share a personal or professional situation that coaching cannot address, your coach is ethically required to ask you to seek a counselor or therapist to help you deal with that issue. Of course, this information (like all coaching information) should be kept confidential.

Ben is a first-year teacher who is working on an alternative licensure path. He is teaching 8th grade social studies and is interested in learning more about the Paideia method. He asks his coach to explain what it is and to help him implement it in his classroom. He is frustrated when his coach suggests he attend a professional development workshop or do some reading about the strategy first.

A coach may have expertise in a certain area and gladly assume a "teaching" role with a teacher or group of teachers. However, this is not part of the traditional coaching role and should not be expected. Coaching doesn't take the place of learning new information. Coaching is about improving what we are doing based on best practices we already know. If you don't have information necessary to implement a new instructional strategy or teach a new concept, then you need to be taught. A coach may suggest workshops, conferences, training sessions, book studies, classroom observations, or personal research. Of course, research (Joyce & Showers, 1995) shows that these forms of professional learning are most effective when supplemented with coaching during implementation and refinement.

What Happens When Trust Is Broken?

Margaret and her coach Doug worked within a norm of understood confidentiality. In a coaching session, Margaret confided to Doug that she really felt she could not work effectively with Pam, her educational assistant, and she intended to go to the principal and ask that Pam be reassigned. A few days later, the principal approached Margaret in the hall and asked to speak with her about her working relationship with Pam. Margaret was furious. Obviously, her coach had talked to the principal.

Unfortunately, this situation is a common one. Reread the vignette. Do we have any evidence that Doug had betrayed Margaret's trust? No, but most of us, like Margaret, might make that inference. Indeed, one of several different things could have happened: (1) the principal could have noticed the problem on her own, without information from the coach; (2) others (perhaps even Pam herself) could have reported the poor relationship to the principal; (3) the coach could have inadvertently betrayed Margaret's confidentiality with a misplaced remark to the principal or someone else who told the principal; or (4) the coach could have intentionally broken his trust with Margaret.

If you believe your coach might have betrayed your trust, your first action should be to have a conversation with your coach. It is unprofessional to make an assumption and end a professional relationship without communicating your reasons. Often, teachers discover that one of the first two previous examples (i.e., the coach did not talk to the principal) is what really happened. Sometimes, they discover that the third scenario (i.e., the coach made a slip of the tongue in an unrelated setting) is what happened.

Indeed, this has even happened to me. In a coaching session, I once heard an observation about a third party. I was so engrossed in thinking about my role as a coach and the teacher I was coaching that I promptly forgot I had heard the comment. A few days later, I made the same comment my teacher had, thinking it was my own observation and not something I had heard in a coaching session. As soon as I discovered what I had done, I went immediately to the teacher, explained my faux pas, and apologized. Fortunately, my relationship with that teacher was strong, she was forgiving, and our relationship was unchanged. If this happened more than once, however, she would be completely justified in backing out of our coaching relationship. Certainly, if a coach intentionally shares confidential information, the coaching relationship is jeopardized and would be difficult to rebuild.

It is imperative that situations such as this are handled with a face-to-face professional conversation when they occur. Both parties should do everything in their power to withhold judgment until they have heard all sides and then be as gracious and forgiving as possible. If a pattern emerges, however, it might be time to end the coaching relationship.

The exception to any expectation of confidentiality is when harm to oneself or others is concerned. Your coach has an ethical obligation to report any harm to yourself or to others (real or threatened) that is revealed in a coaching session.

What Happens When the Budget Won't Allow Coaching?

Ideally, every school should have well-trained, full-time instructional coaches. In reality, funding for coaching programs varies widely from district to district and from school to school. Most of the time, when budget demands dictate, coaching positions are among the first to go. What can a school, a team, or an individual teacher do when the budget is tight and a coaching program is either cut entirely or not implemented at all?

- One district trains every school administrator and all district office personnel (including the superintendent) in coaching. Leaders use coaching skills in their interactions with faculty and parents, and they train their own teachers to coach one another. This provides, over time, a rich institutional understanding that coaching is a leadership strategy that all leaders—whether in the classroom or in the boardroom—can use effectively.
- In another district, the board of education allocated a small stipend to teachers who were willing to give up their planning periods to coach fellow teachers.
- A "turnaround school" received funds to reduce class size to 15, but after a review of the research, decided that raising class size to 20 and hiring a coach for each grade level would do more to decrease teacher turnover and increase teacher efficacy.
- In another school, the coaching position was cut, and the teacher returned to her classroom, but colleagues who had come to depend on coaching asked her to train them. They started coaching one another on their own. Coaching had become such an integral part of the school culture that staff members used it in all of their professional interactions.
- A group of coaches from different school districts met at a coaching conference and decided to exchange phone numbers and begin weekly coaching sessions over the phone. Serendipitously, they improved their own coaching skills as they coached one another!

Important work, such as teaching and coaching, is always subject to the challenges of relationships, trust, time, budgets, and bureaucracies. Fortunately, coaching promotes thinking and can help us identify and develop creative solutions to problems that teachers and coaches encounter as they work together to create a culture of coaching in their schools.

To give your feedback on this publication
and be entered into a drawing for a
free ASCD Arias e-book, please visit
www.ascd.org/ariasfeedback

ASCD | arias™

ENCORE

ADDITIONAL TOOLS AND RESOURCES

Getting to Know Yourself

Getting to know yourself and your coach is a great way to begin a professional relationship. Greater awareness of your learning preferences, temperaments, personality profiles, and work styles can give you both insight into the best ways for you to work together. This information can also help you understand how your own preferences may affect the way you teach students who have different preferences. It is wonderful if you have professional test administration from a licensed counselor available. However, if—like most teachers—you do not, there are some great free or inexpensive inventories available on the Internet.

A free learning-styles quiz is available on the Edutopia website at http://www.edutopia.org/multiple-intelligences-learning-styles-quiz.

The following inventories may be helpful to educators who wish to better understand their own ways of working and learning:

- The Color Code: available with registration at www.colorcode.com.
- HumanMetrics Jung Typology Test: available for free at www.humanmetrics.com.
- Kaleidoscope Profile: available for purchase at www.plsclasses.com/store/resources.

- Myers-Briggs Typology Inventory: information on individual and group administration is available at www.myersbriggs.org. Local universities and employers often offer this testing for free for their students or employees.

Learning More About Coaching

The ICF Code of Ethics and Core Competencies

Even though most schools do not yet require specific credentials for coaching, school coaches are held to the same code of ethics and are expected to have the same minimum competencies as coaches in private practice. The International Coach Federation provides a Code of Ethics that is applicable to all coaches, whether they are working for a school system or for individual clients. Reviewing these ethics and competencies can help a teacher who is being coached understand more about what coaching is and what coaches can and cannot do. Details can be viewed at http://www.coachfederation.org/about/ethics.aspx.

Coaching Structures and Protocols

The coaching conversation must be structured to be effective and time-efficient. Common features of coaching protocols are agreements participants make at the outset and a recap of the conversation and agreements for next steps made at the end. In the middle, there are many different ways to achieve the purpose of the conversation, whether to set goals, solve problems, plan, or reflect. Your coach will likely have a conversation model or frame that he or she learned in training and will share with you. Sometimes, it's helpful to try a new structure in order to expand creativity or get out of a conversation "rut." A few that you may wish to try are listed below; many more are available on the Internet. Alternatively, you may decide to create your own!

- **CLEAR** (Contracting, Listening, Exploring, Action, Review). (Hawkins & Smith, 2006)

In this model, the coach and teacher make a contract with each other by establishing desired outcomes and agreements, use active listening, explore possibilities for future action, choose a next step, and review the decisions made and the value added in the conversation.

- **GROW** (Goals, Reality, Options, Will). (Whitmore, 2002)

The GROW model is one of the best-known models and was used first in athletic coaching. In it, the coach and teacher identify the teacher's goals, clarify the current reality of the situation, identify options for moving forward, and then commit to an option for action in the "What will you do?" phase of the conversation.

- **RESULTS** (Resolve, Establish, Seek, Unveil, Leverage, Take action, Seize success). (Kee, Anderson, Dearing, Harris, & Shuster, 2010)

This model is used by leaders, teachers, and coaches as they work with one another and think individually about their own goals and aspirations. In it, the individual resolves to change, establishes clarity around his or her goals, seeks integrity by matching actions to values and beliefs, unveils multiple pathways, leverages options, takes action, and then seizes success through celebration.

- **SWOT** (Strengths, Weaknesses, Opportunities, Threats). (Easton, 2009)

This model has long been used in business settings, but it is equally effective in education. It can be used to creatively evaluate teaching objectives or analyze problems in the classroom. The coach and teacher identify the problem and the characteristics within the teacher (i.e., strengths) that might help solve that problem. Next, the weaknesses that might hinder success are discussed. Finally, the coach and teacher consider external opportunities that might help and threats that might hinder. This protocol is helpful to differentiate between factors that can and cannot be controlled and to prompt teachers to identify ways to approach those factors they can control (i.e., strengths and weaknesses).

Other Coaching and Professional Learning Protocols

Coaches and teachers often work together in pairs, but coaches can also coach groups or set up teams with members who coach themselves. Either can be done effectively through facilitated teams using protocols (processes) that have shared norms for focusing the conversation and sharing the talking and listening time. The following resources include various protocols and are valuable for teams to use while examining student work and professional practice, addressing problems, and creating effective discussions.

- *National School Reform Faculty Resource Book.* Available from National School Reform Faculty, Harmony Education Center, www.nsrfharmony.org.
- *Protocols for Professional Learning* by Lois Brown Easton (ASCD, 2009).

References

Aguilar, E. (2013). *The art of coaching.* San Francisco: Jossey-Bass.

Annenberg Institute for School Reform. (2004). *Instructional coaching: Professional development strategies that improve instruction.* Providence, RI: Brown University. Available: www.annenberginstitute.org/pdf/InstructionalCoaching.pdf

Biancarosa, G., Bryk, A., & Dexter, E. (2010). Assessing the value-added effects of literacy collaborative professional development on student learning. *The Elementary School Journal, 111*(1), 7–34.

Bruce, C., & Ross, J. (2008). A model for increasing reform implementation and teacher efficacy: Teacher peer-coaching in Grades 3 and 6 mathematics. *Canadian Journal of Education, 31*(2), 346–370.

Easton, L. (2009). *Protocols for professional learning.* Alexandria, VA: ASCD.

Edwards, J. L., Green, K. E., Lyons, C. A., Rogers, M. S., & Swords, M. E. (1998, April). *The effects of cognitive coaching and nonverbal classroom management on teacher efficacy and perceptions of school culture.* Paper presented at the annual meeting of the American Educational Research Association, San Diego, CA.

Hawkins, P., & Smith, N. (2006). *Coaching, mentoring and organizational consultancy: Supervision and development.* Maidenhead, UK: Open University Press.

Joyce, B., & Showers, B. (1995). *Student achievement through staff development: Fundamentals of school renewal* (2nd ed.). White Plains, NY: Longman.

Kee, K., Anderson, K., Dearing, V., Harris, E., & Shuster, F. (2010). *Results coaching: The new essential for school leaders.* Thousand Oaks, CA: Corwin.

Palmer, P. (2007). *The courage to teach: Exploring the inner landscape of a teacher's life, 10th anniversary edition.* San Francisco: Jossey-Bass.

Whitmore, J. (2002). *Coaching for performance.* London: NB Publishing.

About the Author

 **Nina Morel** is an associate professor of education and Director of M.Ed. Programs at Lipscomb University in Nashville, Tennessee. She was a 2005 Milken Educator Award winner and has taught at the middle school, high school, and university levels. She has led ELL and coaching programs for a large school district. Morel is coauthor of *How to Build an Instructional Coaching Program for Maximum Capacity* (Corwin, 2012). Readers may contact her at nina.morel@lipscomb.edu.

The author would like to thank the teachers and coaches in Franklin Special School District (TN), Hampton City Schools (VA), Metro Nashville Public Schools (TN), Robertson County Schools (TN), Rutherford County Schools (TN), and Sumner County Schools (TN) for their contributions.